STRANGE CREATURES

STRANGE CREATURES

ALYSON MILLER

RECENT
WORK
PRESS

Strange Creatures
Recent Work Press
Canberra, Australia

Copyright © Alyson Miller, 2019

ISBN: 9780648404286 (paperback)

 A catalogue record for this
book is available from the
NATIONAL
LIBRARY National Library of Australia
OF AUSTRALIA

All rights reserved. This book is copyright. Except for private study,
research, criticism or reviews as permitted under the Copyright Act,
no part of this book may be reproduced, stored in a retrieval system, or
transmitted in any form by any means without prior written permission.
Enquiries should be addressed to the publisher.

Cover photo by Alexander Krivitskiy on Unsplash
Cover design: Recent Work Press
Set by Charlotte Anderson

recentworkpress.com

Contents

Part 1 Sleeping

Dream animals	1
Sleep	2
Dream babies	3
Thief	4
Incubation	5
Dissection (ii)	6
Butcher	7
Kill floor	8
Gift	9
Skogskyrkogården	10
Metals (ii)	11
Outhouse	12
Wings	13
Road kill	14
Wolf	15
Planarian worms	16
Heterocera	17
Lunar	18
Iron maiden	19
Brothers Grimm	20
Guppy	21
Asylum (i)	22
Asylum (ii)	23

Part 2 Waking

Eugenia	27
Sister-wives	28
Jordgubbe	29
Miyajima	30
Luganville	31
On mountains	32
The twelve dancing princesses	33
The girl who cried wolf	34
Plums	35
On water	36
Shot gun	40
Neck	41
Possessed	42
Animals	43
Fukushima	44
Hunter	45
Tight-locked	46
On hearts	47
Bypass	48
Southerly	49
History	50
Catharsis	51

Part 1

Sleeping

Dream animals

It is four am and the sound of sobbing outside the window pulls us from dreams filled with underwater shapes. For a while, we mistake the noise for a small animal in the gaps between the wood and the insulation, crawling into a heart-space of heat. But then we listen, and the crying turns into a keening that breaks across our whispers, like something ancient has been cut and broken, lost deep in a great sea. In the muted light, something violent unfurls, a sudden fury in which bones meet harder surfaces and glass cracks and falls into driveway gravel like sparks. Then there is sleep, as we are tugged back to unconsciousness before a day hung-over with the shadow of dying things, and the ghostly echo of 'please, please, just let me in, please'.

Sleep

In the landscapes of sleep, he is caked in his body. Thick and heavy with night, his bones unlock themselves, fall loose against muscle and flesh, collapse into the springs of the mattress. Fat tongued, his mouth is huge and cobwebbed—words can't blow through his teeth, but keep catching on lips licked dry against the pillow. His right arm is pinned, the bicep caught under the jaw of a girl. She is curled anemone tight, her breath so close to his skin she might be able to taste salt on each inhale. Somewhere in his wiring an impulse quivers and he twitches, sharply. And then again. Electricity sparked, his arm tenses and jolts upwards, hitting the girl as hard and sudden as hail. She cries out and holds her face like a clue. Blind and unsure, her memory of something violent is a half-thing caught in the sheets, felt for and lost with the shadows on the wall, the first piece of light through the curtains.

Dream babies

It has a full set of teeth and shouts her name. Another rises in her belly like dough in the hours from breakfast to dinner, spilling onto the kitchen floor with a rush of her insides—its naked head blinking and slick against the muscle of her stomach and liver. Some simply appear like a hiccup mid-sentence, crying in her arms as though forever lost and returned home. She forgets their names and their happening, searching the walls of her home for proof of a hoax or a haunting. Or they transform, shape-shifting into horses or beans or dolls, masks on the walls or reflections that speak memories of thimbles and shadows. And then the ghost child, an infant of smoke and glass that holds to her like guilt even as she screams and claws and tries to pluck it from her skin. In the darkness of early morning, they gather around her bed like homunculi, whispering *mater matris, mater matris, mater matris,* pressing the words into her sleep and burying them bone-deep.

Thief

He watches them sleep, holding his breath before the dead weight of their night bodies, as though hunting. He scans her face the hardest, notes the shadows that turn white skin into a horror mask of sunken eyes and wet teeth, the pink tip of tongue, warm, sour air. An animal face, hints of bone and darkness. Against her belly, the tight ball of a cat, ears twitching with rabbit visions and the minutiae of sounds only heard in those curious hours before light. He takes a pillow and holds it firm to her mouth and nose; feels only a single kick of protest before the smell of earth and ammonia. He drops the cat into a canvas bag and parcels it under his arm, squeezing its soft gut against his ribs. He leaves the room humming, the vibrations filling his ears and throat with the melody of underwater dreams.

Incubation

Incandescent, the face is alien bright, cocooned in an amniotic dream space of heartbeats and echolocation. The outside, that other world that taps across the surface of her belly like some ancient code, tries to imprint upon a neophyte whose cells are wired only for survival: the battle noise of Wagner; the poetry of the dead. And it is parasitical, burying deep into the viscera of its carrier, into the gut and the marrow, sucking and clawing for food. On the monitor, phalange scrape at her ribs and spine, searching. It feels the pulse of the cardiac muscle, the steady race of blood entering the atrium, then the ventricle, pumped into pulmonary circulation, hunting oxygen. The rhythmic thud is hypnotic, like some primitive language; a summons in a ritual of devourment. And so it crawls upwards, drinking adrenalin and curiosity, aware only distantly of hormones flooded with the bitter smell of pain; the metallic taste of fear.

Dissection (ii)

Parts of the bowel were found first, congealed in the blood-sticky path to the bedroom. It had been shredded with patient ferocity, the meaty tissue tinged with that curious red-purple of erections, malar flush, and the dehydrated bodies of Echeveria recurvata. A cleaver hung snug in the headboard, as though caught mid-sentence, the words buried in the hard wood, splinter-deep. The sheets bore terrible witness, the fabric gorged thick with escaped organs, shit-stained yet taut across the mattress—ready for the penny-bounce, hospital corners were origami crisp. He was inside me when he attacked, she said, so I went inside him, tugged it all out. She was found in the street, naked and blood-drenched, his intestines around her shoulders like an adornment in a pagan ritual. I just hung on, she said, reached deep and pulled, like drawing up an anchor, hauling fish from the sea.

Butcher

A counter of glass and steel so bright she cannot help but stare into the red spaces of her face, like something gynecological—the startle of a beaked speculum, the surprise of gloved hands searching inwards. The window is frocked with oily rows of goose-bumped ducks, thick straps of stripped tender pink lamb, grey intestinal worms of sausage. The naked body of a suckling pig stretches along the counter like a pornographic invitation, its stomach zippered open to expose crisp ribs through creamy layers of porcelain white fat. Its face is as round and full as a boy's, the wet baby eyes blackened and small. An apprentice weighs the heft of a short cleaver—and the head gives way, the nose squashed against the cool clean tiles like resignation, or a kiss.

Kill floor

That day, a kid runs loose, hooves clack-clicking against the slick concrete. It falls, and the fat white underbelly is stained with scarlet, hind legs spraddled achingly wide. Bleach-wetted walls stream with the heat of newly stilled bodies on the belt; the air heaves with blood and ammonia. It bleats a horror cry, and in its milk-pale eyes, there is you, an image of a rubber-clothed man, kneeling. Your throat is choke-tight, and the room is a test, a locked box of quantum superposition. In the madness of the echo-chamber, the kid butts against your arm, horn-buds crusted with viscera and shit, its hot tongue flapping and bloated. You pull it to your chest, feel its wild heart thrash with your own; its wet breath is hard against your cheek as you stand, count to ten, and walk towards the door.

Gift

That two am caterwaul, the one somehow both deep and pitched to reach the innermost ear. The gift, a palm-small sack of bird, its feathers so young they haven't yet hardened with flight or night cold or the alchemy of powderdowns. A nervous twitch in a twig leg is only a confidence trick; the opened chest is spit-clean, consumed with the suck and lick of slurping oysters or milk. Its wooden beak kisses your thumb, the hollowed body nestling inside your enormous hand like a sacrifice or tribute. I carve out a sparrow-sized grave in the garden, beneath the acrid bite of marigolds, the orange globes meaty and wet above dark winter dirt. In the morning, thick with fatigue and thoughts of work, you find a nest on the driveway, the chalky white shells of its contents cracked and sticky on the bricks. Inside the window, the cat sleeps, a dead weight.

Skogskyrkogården

In the half-light, we walk through woodlands that keep lost children and old stones, shadowed by pines that seem to breathe small prayers into the wind. Joggers weave silently around tombstones like night creatures and we stare at them like exotic and unreal things. By a bunker that once stored bodies but now stores potatoes, we hear of how a girl died playing hide and seek among the graves, knocked by a falling headstone into cold sleep; folded into the dirt. And how, undone by the curious death, the people of the surrounding village laid flat the remaining stones like a ritual, pulling them out like old teeth and wrapping them back into the safety of earth.

Metals (ii)

On a street that smells like fresh grass and packed lunches, she watches an old couple tumble across the road, moving away from something unseen, but heard. The sound falls against the window, a violence of words that hits the glass and strikes the couple now crouching behind the letterbox, holding plastic bags full of groceries to their chests. A man, or maybe a woman, skeletal and dressed in virgin white, moves down the footpath like something haunted, hunted, a long sword in one hand; a machete in the other. Behind the curtain she listens hard, wondering what the old man is whispering to his wife, her round face caught between his palms so firmly her mouth is trapped, wet and fish-like. They are safe in this moment. From the radio, the hourly news exhales into the room, punctuated by the echo of a growl, a shouted fuck, and the ghostly ring of metal moving through the air.

Outhouse

She peels down her knickers and lifts her skirts, feels the sticky contact of the plastic toilet seat and thinks of the other bodies here before her, sweltering. In the corner, there is a family of mice, sweet and musty, buried in an abandoned pile of magazines. She pushes a toe into the nest, catches a glimpse of the jellybean babies, eyes mute, skin tacky and damp. Their neophyte skin is translucent, grotesque—for a moment, she must swallow the urge to break open their tiny skulls. The bullet noise of rain chases out the thought, rich petrichor mingling with dirt and sulfur. She places her fingertips against the metal, feels the shock burst of cool air against her legs. A thin line of rainwater trickles onto the magazines; the mice dig deep, holing their way through the paper as though racing to the centre of the earth.

Wings

A woman and a child on a street greasy with the aftermath of rain; slug-heavy flowerheads on the pavement. He points upwards, to a bat hanging from power lines, the patagium biting hard into the threads of hot wire. Its belly is ash coloured and full, moon-like over feet bent into arthritic shapes. He wants to stroke the leather membrane of its wings while she is reminded of a jilted Chinese bride who dressed in the ruched silk and tulle of her wedding gown and stepped from a window in mimicry of flight. Caught by the neck, her body hung like a lace-shrouded Lepidoptera from the arm of a stranger. The boy, compelled by the weird flesh displayed above his head, points to the broken teeth and black eyes of the bat, murmuring words about electricity and death, and the curious dreaming of animals.

Road kill

On a road next to a dark flick of tyre, a headless kangaroo. Slumped into the asphalt as though fallen mid-leap into sleep, the body angles out like a lambda. Inside it is a child with transparent skin and vacuum eyes, wondering at the sudden break in its mother's blood rhythms. Held tight between bitumen, darkness and cooling flesh, the baby life, bean small, coagulates. Against light the colour of toffee that turns traffic into martian shapes, the silhouette of the corpse is barely there. Gum tree shadows pull them into the dark, and the night is enormous.

Wolf

On the grass, a rabbit bakes in the sun. Its jumper has been torn free, and a ginger cat pulls at the hind leg, red raw and twisted through with hard muscle. From the verandah, the smell of chalk and burnt paper, and the acrid smack of a cigarette held for too long. The sound of gravel friction as a sliding door opens and radio noise escapes, let loose into air touched only by birds and rain storms. Inside, at a table frocked in red gingham, a man prises open a laptop like a dentist parting lips and teeth. Pushing a silver disc into the narrow slit, his face is caught in the screen light like something unknown. Sound muted, the bodies before him jerk like marionettes, angular and doll-small. Outside, the first trail of ants thread the body of the doe. Stripped open to the skies, the small snubbed jaw of its face is as pink as a kiss.

Planarian worms

Under the floorboards in a womb-space, there are four children, hunched and translucent like planarian worms. Trapped in the weight of the dark earth, they sing lullabies and recite fairytales in the heavy air, always in half-breaths as they listen for the sound of movement on the stairs. The odd flicker of light speaks maybe of food or some new game to play, or those other things too large for words. Their mother-sister hums an old Austrian carol, remembering the voices of the choirs her children and siblings might never hear: *still, still, still, weil's Kindlein schlafen will.* As she sings, she thinks of her eldest, who has taken to plucking out her hair and shredding her dresses, stuffing the fabric into the toilet until its porcelain throat is choked. She cannot help her. *Wenn wir einmal sterben müssen, wir, wir, wir, wir rufen all zu dir.*

Heterocera

There are moths in the sheets, tangled in the pilled cotton like insinuations and old stains. Hooked into the fabric, the thick thorax cones of their bodies seem woven into the linen like broderie anglaise, whirling floral patterns of insect life. No beating will shake them out; nestled in wardrobes, their spindle legs emerge along collars and hemlines like whispers and plague. *Aglossa cuprina* are as feared as nightmares; the grease moth that feeds on the rendered fat of humans. The dirty cousins of the lepidopteron family, multiplication is no chore, and each generation finds its way with the one before. Inside, the walls have disappeared under the woolly mass of their weight; a world turned twilight for their crepuscular preferences. Outside, the *Attacus atlas*, fed on fertilizers and hormones in the rain, grow bat-large and territorial, nerve-endings wired for celestial navigation. And they circle, endlessly, the millions whose names mimic the gods—Luna, Polyphemus, Atlas, Promothea—guided by the sun, then the moon, for the promise of a straight-line home. In the gardens, there are only bones now, skies choked in a veil of paper-thin wings and the gentle plummet of corpses that flew too high.

Lunar

During the Harvest Moon, he says, dog bites are twice as common, something about the magic of the lunar cycle and lycanthropy and the canine tug of the cosmos. He says it's about opposites, the hemisphere of the moon facing off against the sun, a difference of 180 degrees, he says, not to forget the synodic month, 29.53 days, but the relevance is hard to remember when you stare into that orange peel surface in the night sky, the brightness a mystery against a blackness that promises only a vacuum of space, and a suffocating memory of eternity. He says it's the beauty of science to fall in love with composites of hydrogen and helium that burn so hard your bones evaporate before your skin gets close, and yet give no warmth to a universe that freezes because there are no molecules against which to bounce; conduction, convention, radiation, he says, which are words that bite in the wet spaces of your mouth. It's -270.45 Celsius out there, he says, which is -454.81 Fahrenheit and you're not sure, because you're still trapped in knowing that heat is also a kind of cold, like a fever from an infection, or a wound.

Iron maiden

A New York subway in summer: a ten-metre vivisection of an intestine that winds endlessly on beneath the steel and stone of the city. The heat is an oil slick, heavy with sweat and the touch of strangers, bodies creeping away from other hips and knees, wet breath on the backs of necks. On the lip of the platform, a milk pale girl, peering into the gaping mouth, the flicker of lights like teeth briefly bared on tiled walls. There is a gash eaten into the hollow of her cheek, blooming with warmth and infection. Blood freckles the collar of a summer frock, elbows torn as though ripped against nails or asphalt. In the roar of the tomb-space, air displaced in the rush of metal and energy, the crowd surges like a murmuration, flesh twisting through the hurry of automatic doors. And she falls away, contracting through the iron maiden like some spirit pulled back into the bottle. In the suck of the exit, she is captured for a moment in the interlocking bars as though anatomized; her body riven, and disappeared.

Brothers Grimm

A story, like a fairytale. Two blind brothers, bound by the intimacy of detail: the smell of sunlight on glass, the weight of air in the winter, the exact height of each door. They are identical in every way. Fingernails: chewed to the quick. Facial hair: a scratching of stubble along the jaw. Eyes: 25 blinks a minute, always. We will not know their names but hear of their bodies on the news and talk for a while about their deaths. We imagine the beautiful town of their home, a village tasting of labyrinthine streets, blue skies, and the clarity of church bells. We listen of the brothers being told that their ears are curling away from the world, rejecting the distress of sound in the same way as their eyes refused the violence of sight. And how, in the same way as grieving whales throw off the weight of the ocean, they gave it all up. Breath: stopped hard in the same gasp. Heads: an awkward fall to the right. Toes: scrunched tight like fists under white sheets.

Guppy

A girl searching in the shadows for a wolf finds a story. Hears the words strung up as neat as teeth and swallows them in, rib-deep. Pressing hard against the sharpness of bones, the story sleeps, but she stays awake. Ears open to clues in the murmurs of trees and bed sheets. In her dreams, narratives float like the cobwebs between fence posts, and she nets them, swallows them deep and feels them kick down her throat into the cavern of her belly. In the day world of traffic lights and train station queues, she searches for more and gulps them in, mouth wide and lips stretched as though pushed against glass. She bloats with adultery and a broken shoe and childhood and a bad day and a friend of a friend and a moment last Friday and a funny thing that happened on the way to work and a coincidence and a memory and guilt. Stories crush into the spaces between her vertebrae, the cracks inside knuckles, the gaps under her nails. For some time, there is only the enormity of their weight pressing skin-tight inside her. And then she is gone, broken up with the violence of escape, of words exploding back into the secrets of tongues and stairwells and sleep.

Asylum (i)

In the hallway, she holds her breath, waiting for the voice again that calls from there, and just there. In a white nightdress she is a ghost, feeling the walls as though they are faces, locked tight with stories. In slippers and night silence, she strains for a whisper that says 'hello, how are you?' and reminds her not to put cans in the microwave, or to fall asleep in her chair, or to forget that the most important things have been, and are going. Somewhere in a drawer, there is a letter that contains delicate things, and some words about gardens and the weather. She calls a name and then cries it, trying to force it into the paintwork like an indent, a foothold.

Asylum (ii)

Shadowed by the highway and its alien lights, you might believe a girl stands in the window, her face kissing the glass as she contemplates a dream as vivid as orange peel and ammonia, the first hit of morning cold: bloody hands on a bridal gown. And a child, hanged by a rope of her own hair, porphyria red. Framed as though photographed, she emerges in the half-light, and speaks to you of the darkness of hallways and locked doors before disappearing in a blink. In a memory, her ghosting seems to recite whispers about inmates whose horrors scrape and drag along the stone walls, beautiful and destructive like tornadoes.

Part 2

Waking

Eugenia

The courts judged her a killer. Found that Eugenia, discovered not as a man but as a woman, murdered poor Annie. The wife who never guessed—until she did. Found that Eugenia cracked open her love's head like some dark place and then burned away the face and lungs, leaving nothing but ribs and the memory of flesh. The jury waited only to know how bodies stripped clean and bare like bones and teeth and eyes left room for tricks and guesses. They eyed the wooden dildo, dangled by its leather strap like a metronome, and thought of women and warm sheets and the weight of breath on skin—and of their own cocks, tucked neatly under buttons and zips. And then Eugenia, the creature in a white linen dress, the animal lost behind circus stories and a gun in her portmanteau: *I do not know anything at all.*

Sister-wives

That trace under the ridge of collarbone, a milky sweet scent not her own. It grows with the warmth of the room, the heat of touch-sticky skin under yellow-stained sheets. It is her night but small invasions burrow bone-deep; those alien hairs that creep across the pillowcase, a menthol smack of toothpaste. His body is stitched tight with other teeth and tongues, with whispers that speak of god and ecstasy and the sanctity of sisters, held fast by inexhaustible cock and childbirth. Her womb is a communal space, occupied by other wives and the strange pulses of embryonic creatures, scratching for light. As a child, her mother slapped her legs for eating the last apple, stinging flesh a lesson against gut and heart. When he's inside her, their ribs locked, her mouth licks against the jugular artery, tracing the thick neck root like a map-line, or a promise. She fights the urge to bite, to choke throat-full of viscous, tangy metal. In the morning, she strips the bed, bleaches linen calcium-white in scorching sun.

Jordgubbe

By a lake in a town that has a name you kiss to say, we eat strawberries, fleshy *jordgubbe* in cardboard pots leaching sticky red. They taste only as maybe they could in Sweden, in that time with that sun; the toothy grin of half-demolished buildings on the Jönköping horizon, the smacking of waves against the pier. Close, some swimmers feel the cold hit their bones, screaming like murder as their toes touch fingers of weed reaching up from the mud and sand. Our hands are stained, the meat of the fruit wedged underneath our fingernails and in between our teeth, and from somewhere is the sound of a gull crying on the breeze.

Miyajima

A mid-morning ferry, the sky slug-grey, the cold wrapped round the knuckle-bones of hands and spines and toes. The shush-hush of puffer jackets and plastic bags, the heave and pull of bodies along Omotesando, drawn by the sick-sweet sponge of Momiji chokefull of red bean or cheese. The smack of salt and brine, of fist-fat oyster flesh burning on grills on footpaths slick with greasy heat and the curious tang of smoking oil. The flicker-ripple of *noren* and the blank stares of *Daruma* waiting for wishes and a pupil pop of colour. At Itsukushima, a bad fortune is left behind, the rice paper kanji tied along wires between shrine pillars, left to rot in the wind like tiny garrotted dancers. Doe-eyed Sika deer sleep beneath gnarlrooted trees, knob-kneed and thick-bellied, the sacred messengers of the gods. By the boat terminal, crowds of women in kimono emerge from doorways in sudden bloom, threading among school children and backpacks like fish or sound. For a moment after the whistle-blow, the body-heavy pier undulates like some living thing, an octopean arm trapped forever between the water and the dirt.

Luganville

Off the boat, and the memory of water is still in our legs. Spat out on the shoreline, the liner watches us spill across the beach like a birth, pouring bright and fast from its insides. A hulking matryoshka. On the road there is a girl with two red bows in hair knotted into plaits and pulled tight between frangipanis and curls. Above her, a woven arch offers a boundary for photographers captured by her smile. Better than a postcard, she is real. Before her, two sea birds perch on a stand, still and blank in a pose that suggests they might not truly be there, while behind her, a less beautiful sister holds a crayon-coloured umbrella and nods towards the box at their feet. 50 metres away, boys sprint to the ocean from a concrete pier, chasing a tyre washed clean in salt and smoothed by coconut husks and coral. We ask to take their picture, and they pull gangster attitudes from other worlds. Hurrying us away with *thank you, thank you, goodbye,* they push us back to the mother ship that has swallowed the horizon.

On mountains

The mute light of morning, the air a deadweight pressed against lungs and chests. We breathe as though under water, clothes sweat-thick, wandering streets and bridges heaving with green life and commuters and the dull ding-ding of narrow trams. Down a street with no name there is a staircase with no end, stone and steep and as crooked as old teeth or my mother's hands. We climb and the city is lost to the mountain, punctuated by road workers pouring bitumen in sticky toffee pools, viscous and night-black. A line of school girls in immaculate white pass in single-file, dresses edged in Mary blue, and disappear into the fog like an illusion or sacrifice, a memory of lost virgins and haunted peaks. A red taxi creeps upwards, past a jogger whose wet skin steams, his body shrouded in haze as though halo-wrapped, or partly erased. The way down is by a spitting sewage pipe, a tunnel trail lined with office windows and washing posts, limp shirts and socks like *memento mori*, a catalogue of domestic ghosts. In a 7/11 later on, a drunken ex-pat warns against the back streets and highland paths and alleyways: the cats are all feral, he says, and strange things are spoken between the wind and the trees.

The twelve dancing princesses

Their parents blamed a toxic conspiracy, something about chemicals creeping through the bedrock like a stain. Claimed it must be under the football field, poisons triggered by cheerleaders and runners punctuating the earth with the regularity of typewriters and bird song. Experts held the mystery as far away as continents, spitting out scripts for antibiotics and hysteria like seeds and broken teeth. On the television, the girls jerked as though possessed, necks and faces pulled hard into alien angles, voices annexed by unreal things. And the symptoms spread like a haunting, an enigma of muscle and some cerebral ghost that eluded X-rays and journalists and psychiatry. The small town, nervous of the water table and porous quarry rocks, shuttered down as tight as an eyelid. And the girls, locked in their rooms and skins, searched night skies and the patterns of leaf falls for some hint of return.

The girl who cried wolf

Ocean town. A girl, lips stitched as tight as a fist. The thread is worm-thick and tarmac-black, fibres woven through with the bite of salt and iron. Inside her mouth, pushing against palate and mucosa, she heaves up words that slip back down her throat like eels. In streets neat as trellis and algebra, the townsfolk chase the ones that get loose, weighing them down in hessian sacks with stones, burying them sea-deep. In the main drag, under neon signs and mannequin stares, a corpse row bleaches in the sun—the smell of sulfur, and a strange sweetness. No one speaks, listening only for the runaways shouting paragraphs and plot endings down alleyways and behind doors. The girl, caged in the town square, circled by a silent mob, plucks at her hair like a penance. But the crowd, tired of the wolf-shapes made by her words, only tightens. Mute as walls, they disappear her into fragments, leaving the smell of burnt paper and a slick of dark ink. Scouring, they gather the scraps and distribute them like a communion, lost fingernails and whisper-thin bones, to be buried under the thresholds of their homes as a memory. A warning.

Plums

Not the ones from the poem, in an icebox, but those from a friend, a delivery in sag-heavy cardboard, nestled among zucchini and spinach like Langshan fowl eggs. Her garden spat forth like some biblical orgy while ours, wind-whipped and paved with tiles and tin, only gasped with the dead choke of weeds. The plum flesh was thick and dark, the skin glaucous; chewing the meat as though eating some animal, gnawing a finger through to the knuckle-ribbed bone. It reminded me of that time cutting pomegranates, the knife that slipped across the red-purple rind and into my finger, carving away the wet tip that scattered with the gem seeds like a mock sarcotesta. Stains that might have been blood or juice wouldn't wash out from your shirt or that porous spot on the bench; but thrown out on the grass, birds pecked clean the fibrous white guts of the fruit.

On water

i.

It's hard not to imagine the time-locked moments of those two spaces: the first, the seconds after the car tore a road past the crumbled jetty end, hovering for only nine thousand million periods of radiation of the caesium atom before collapsing against the surface of the sea like a drunk into uncertain liquid dreams. The second, those minutes during equalization as the water chugged into the passenger space and the open mouths of children wrapped safety-tight in booster seats, cocooned from oncoming traffic but not the madness of a driver who could not block the sirens from his ears. And afterwards, beneath the neatly geometrical phrases of newspapers and journalists, an image: their tiny bodies crammed full of ocean, floating as though bottled, arms raised towards the screaming of tyres and gulls and tourists, the red wet sacks of their lungs exploding with salt and fear.

ii.

The suitcase washes up first, on a Monday, its grey blue skin scudding onto the shorelines of Lake Traunsee. It contains the purple white parts of a wife with no name, chopped parcel-small and bundled into the travel bag that used to hold old towels frayed by the scrape of wet bodies and the metal belly of the washing machine. Opened by tourists, the sodden flesh of her torso is newly alive with water worms and crabs as pale and pink as fingernails. On Tuesday, divers emerge with a husband of no name, whose limbs are woven around baggage knotted tight to ankles and wrists in a caricature of an octopus or bladderwrack weed. Hanging from the right shoulder, wrapped in a cool slate casing of concrete, is the head of his wife. A rope screwed into the outer shell, she draggles like a Christmas bauble or treat, an imperfect Siamese twin. In the folklore of Salzkammergut, a region whose sound echoes the cut and choke of Seppuku, legends tell of a hippocamp ridden by a grieving mermaid; a lake monster tied to a beautiful suicide, or the reverse. In the cases anchoring his body to the silt and mud of the waterbed, forensics find a pulpy mess of letters; a bag of baby teeth and needle-thin fish bones; and the soft ears of a knitted yellow bear.

iii.

There is traffic mobbed across the bridge, the one that almost gave up before it was finished, the steel mass of its belly kissing into the soft mud of the riverbanks. Vivisected by the geometry of iron and concrete, cables and girders cut into the sky as cars and trucks crawl towards the fume-soaked darkness of the tunnel, nose to tail like animals sniffing and nudging their way into the bowels of the ark. The heat is as combustible as tempers and kindling, the promise of a southerly as distant and foreign as flight. At the apex, a man stands against the railing, holding a doll-small girl over the smack of water below, both as still as the instance between heartbeats. It seems a cruel game until the drop, the tiny body trapped in that liminal space between falling and landing, a time that is both forever and nothing. As he returns to the car, arms emptied, there is only the screaming of gulls, and the weight of breath held, of pulses thrashing against throats and wrists.

iv.

The roof cuts the surface at first, a black slick mirroring the cord rush and tangle weeds as though nestling in for the hunt. It is an autumn sky, the water edged with the orange and gold of hibernation and decay, the shocks of red foliage a warmth like lust or infection. On equalizing, open windows gape like greedy mouths, dragging it all inside, but the car floats with the thick calm of drowsing. The prosecution says she unbuckled on acceleration, unwound from the seat to swim clear as the lake sucked in the weight of steel and flesh, drawing the heat of engines and blood into its belly before spitting them out, washed clean. Tethered, her children are compressed, left blind by the pressure of silt and swell. Air bubbles through their clothes like hope; the promise of rising. The screams echo for days, a threnody trapped between the reeds and the gulls.

Shot gun

The police say he was provoked. That she waved an angry black cock at him, the shaft as long as the blue-veined space between her wrist and elbow. It was found later, under a table near an old nappy, the cat and forty kilograms of aluminum cans. Across the grass field, crackle dry, the track curled like a hook into the trees holding the perimeter. Car tyres spat gravel as she reversed and he followed, and she couldn't help but watch his face. The image would almost have been beautiful but for the screaming of the gearbox and the breathless silence of the sky.

Trapped tight as a plait against blackberries that had refused to burn, she wound up her window. In the trees—old gums with white and peeling skin—there were flashes of blue, and wet mouths, red with urgent words. He walked to the side of the car, the taste of iron on his teeth and in the air. He shattered the glass and then her skull and then his own. From his pocket, the sound of ringing went on and on. And then there was nothing.

Neck

The streets are swept over with the small invasions of early autumn—swathes of leaves torn free from branches like scabs or plucked hairs; the odd cicada shell, its body crawled elsewhere. Through the suburbs, they thread their way coastal, forgetting maps and relying only on the smell of the briny shoreline for guidance, like the celestial navigation of moths, or Darwin's dead reckoning. A line of ocean appears, guarded by gulls screaming like newborns in the glass-still air. On the beach, a carpet-brown dog nuzzles seaweed, emerging with the dull corpse of a sea bird, its feathers scant and tattered. Through the car window, she watches as a woman dressed in the greens and blues and greys of an oil slick tears the creature away, throws it into the sea, only for the dog to follow, desperate to rescue its wet treasure, to nurse it between eager paws. Tenderly, it licks the hard-beaked head, but drunk on the scent of salt and sulfur and mineral, forgets its love; bites through the tender neck.

Possessed

Some say that when a cat adopts that lock-eyed vacuum stare into the impossible space behind you, it can see the ghosts that crawl along ceilings and walls; that it is captured by the smoky entrails of invisible bodies. Others argue for the minutiae of insects; the patterns dappled into the eggshell surface of the paintwork; the micro-currents cutting across the floorboards. Online we discover prosencephalon disease, rabies and toxic poisoning, encephalitis, parasites and hepatic encephalopathy, an invasion of nerve-endings and circuitry that mistakes tumors for prophecy. And then you, with that gaze as steady as buildings and dancers and my father's hands, a look that promises to work its way inside us like a virus, or a dream. We tell stories of possession and cuckoos; discover the Sumerian *ashipu*, those sorcerers trained in luring out the sickness demons. But understanding the strange knowledge of children and cats, we burn herbs in every corner, laughing; and at night, as you sleep in a confusion of fur and skin, we take the knives from the kitchen, lock the door to your room.

Animals

A foal collapses out of its mother and takes a mouthful of dry earth, thick dirt scratching its teeth. The mare backs into the shade of ghost gums, drags an ear against the chalky bark as though trying to erase it. The suffocating thrum of crickets, scavengers buried in paddocks beaten flat by blackberries and sunken fence lines. In the afternoon sun, the foal is autumn-coloured, blushed with patches of something that reveal the science has not sparked true. In the evening, under a low potato moon, the shadow of a man falls across the grass, a metre of pipe held tight against his side. Locusts spray out with each footfall, darting away like dark electricity. The screaming of horses cracks open the night.

Fukushima

The bodies of the wild boars have to be broken into pieces before burning, the furnaces gagging with the parts of only three a day. They cannot be buried; dogs hustle into the dark ground for flesh and bone. Leached with radium and grief the wool-thick pigs trample the wastelands, black-snouted monsters from some dystopic dream. A local entombed a carcass in the garden, letting it rot within warm layers of clay and dirt. In the spring, the rib cage curled from the soil like an awakening, a thoracic whisper of silence and death. It will be 30 years before the daikon grow without mutation, while the boar breed like tuber crop in the red zone. Hunters reduce the herd, put hog hair into their pockets for luck, but no one will volunteer to wrap the beasts within the fire. It is the last animal of the zodiac, *yama kujira*, the mountain whale. There is not enough room for the corpses, spat out on hillsides like preternatural seeds; the earth will eat us all slowly.

Hunter

The gym, midsummer. Suffocation of sweat and rubber. The chlorinated tang of metal and sperm. The steady dud-dud of music, syncopating puff-breaths and heavy-lift moans. Gull-like screams from the pool beyond. A distant voice counting, over and over. A man in front of her, knitted tight with the anabolic pop of muscle and sinew. Quadriceps bulging as though small animals slept inside, hugging to bone. About 55kgs, he says, around the same as the doe-bambi-deer from the hunting. Give or take, depending on hydration. I've got a bullseye, he says, and a dead body doesn't weigh more, rigor mortis just makes it harder to lift, he says. Bleed and gut first, he says, and always freeze the flesh, because of the parasites. Fat-fingered fists grip the treadmill. Run faster than a shot, he says. Behind him, rapid-fire mouths open and shut on a muted television; she watches their teeth. A dumbbell drops; a cry of pain leaks into the empty spaces and he is gone.

Tight-locked

The windows were tight-locked, aluminum frames shut against winter and puberty and a northerly that banged against the surface like Cathy returning from the moors. Mould tracked the glass like veins, sucked close to corners and fed by closed-breath and blocked light and the steady thrum of ducted heating. A hermetic space, nothing out, nothing that might crawl inside the dark places of memory and sleep. We unwound those screws, broke open the circulation of a room sealed by a father's fear of a daughter who would not speak, of a story of a next-door man who looked upon children with too much love. The sill grooves were earth-jammed and corpse-filled, slaters and silver moths and fat black flies whose maggots had long departed, their bodies leach-dry. Ovoviviparous, you say, larvae hatching inside the mother, a nightmare of birth and devourment. We scrub the metal over and over, fingers bone-sodden with bleach and hot water. Under the ledge, initials are gouged into the white painted wood in a language we cannot read, the deep strikes like a trapped witness, a haunted voice from a dream.

On hearts

It started with stomach flu, your body leached crackle-dry. A night and day of heaving, crouched before the porcelain neck of the toilet as acid burned your throat raw, bleached the calcium from your teeth. In the hours before morning, pulse thrashing like trapped fish and convinced something alien is attempting birth from your chest, you ask me to Google *symptoms of cardiac arrest, cardiopulmonary failure* and, to be sure, *indigestion*. In the ER, imaging reveals only a fissure, a rib-torn muscle that will soon knit bone-tight. On leaving, the streets vacant with that brief desolation of night and heavy with petrichor, we talk of magnetic fields and radio waves, the intimacy between gut and heart, and the impossible magnetics of hydrogen atoms.

Bypass

The heart is the core, even though it is off-centre and so close to the throat. Its beating is a haunting, travelling the arterial lines into ears and mouths, awakening in the twitch of a bicep; that patient thrum in your gut. Yours was broken, not guitar string snapped like a wailing country song, but a heaving grey slug choking against your chest and lungs. The surgeon made no promises but like a good electrician, sought to tighten the loose connections. Your body was unzipped, ribs cracked wide like wings to frame the faulty organ, a parody of a memorial tattoo. Inside the wet purple space, doctors made note of the curious erosion of those tissues knitted by secrets and the compulsions of the living, worn away by decades of hard use. It takes five grafts to rebuild the pathways of blood and oxygen to keep the perpetual rhythm: the sinoatrial node transmitting through the atria to the antrioventricular and so on, bio-mechanics the solution to it all. Later, fat fingered and drug woozy, you wandered the halls like a Christmas ghoul, wailing like a newborn as you prophesized the hopes of a new world.

Southerly

A night of prowling hallways, the wind tugging at the roof like some Baumian nightmare. You lock windows and doors, close curtains and blinds against the wailing of a southerly that worms inside our ears and bones like madness or infection. You're afraid it won't hold, that the tin sheets will peel like burnt skin from our box-neat home and reveal the insides, as pink and raw as baby mice. In the early hours, you talk of your father's body, of muscle and stone chewed up by fat and despair, remembering that time his heart had to be scraped clean. Its arrhythmic lub-dub never settled to the safekeeping of children and houses, its chamber rooms clogged slug-thick with secrets and whiskey and love songs. By morning, the garden a devastation of gum tree trash and snapped-leg sparrows, you have learned the names of exotic winds. Walking the outside perimeter, you chant into the gasped-out air: *khamseen, gibli, xlokk, föhn, shamal*. A neighbour hears your poem, takes his dogs inside, bolt-locks the door.

History

That night going the long way, round the back-roads with the real gardens and the old people's home and the footpaths twisted like broken teeth and drunkenness and that lie you told the day before. All Saint's Eve, choked with allergies and lost bees and milk-pale skin and the promise of heat. There had been too much garlic in the *moo nham tok*, not enough chili in the *gang massaman*. You took photos of a grape vine seeded in a rotted pipe, the clusters of green fruit dick-shaped and hard and bitter. At the bus-stop, a woman asked the time; she had to lay flowers at the cemetery for a husband who survived the Holocaust but not the flu, who died hot and aching and tired. You worried about her fumbling around tombstones on an evening for undead things, and she told you she's nearly there, that the tock-tick of limbs was slowing to the stutters of a heart filled with ghouls. At the end, she said, small things will catch you, worm inside like a black thought and fill up the spaces between memory and bone. In the morning, you found a bush rat on the front lawn, its little body matted thick with brown ants and flies. You buried it beneath the jasmine, ribs skywards, pink belly split wide, and tucked in the dirt like a benediction, a blessing for the safety of the ground.

Catharsis

A bone-shaker roar, throwing the birds from house beams, rippling soft plaster walls like fabric or fingers or water. We woke from half-dreams, tripping down floorboards with nuclear images flaring behind sluggish eyes, the resounding boom-bass a promise of death-makers and flattened earth and retribution. The noise echoed from the toilet, a gut-deep belch rebounding from the tiles, the bowl a giant wet mouth of anguish and sulphurous gas. We couldn't breathe, ears and noses plugged with a smell of rot so thick it might be cut out of the empty spaces between us. The cistern seized in epileptic rumbling, liquid streaming from the tank as though weeping. We reached for towels, bricks, and spanners as the choked porcelain throat spewed out a deluge of all that was lost: a baby doll, a Russian novel, a speckle-cracked cup. The clasp of a shoe, the lid of a pen, the old shelf that used to hold pictures, the odd glass. Flooded with battered, broken things, the viscera of history and disappointment and love. We fought for air and light, retching in fumes and the weight of objects that heaved from forgotten places. Enveloped, we held fast to the ceramic belly of the latrine, took it all in, and waited for morning.

Afterword

According to Kafka, 'we ought to only read the kind of books that wound or stab us. If the book we're reading doesn't wake us up with a blow to the head, what are we reading for? ... We need books that affect us like a disaster, that grieve us deeply, like the death of someone we loved more than ourselves, like being banished into forests far from everyone, like a suicide'. Such a violent vision of the reading experience suggests an argument against pleasure or comfort, but also reveals something about the need to be moved, transformed in perhaps unutterable, unspeakable ways. The same might also be said of the process of writing, which demands nothing if not an ability to recognise the frightening strangeness of that which appears most familiar; a perspective which has the tendency to unearth the macabre nature of the every day. The poems in this collection seek, if not to wound a lá Kafka, then at least to unsettle by grappling with real-world instances of taboo through the reconstruction of surreal and traumatic events. By concentrating on that which discomforts, *Strange Creatures* is an attempt towards understanding acts of violence—both domestic and extra-ordinary—as well as the prohibited, especially in relation to death, sexuality, and instances of extreme or unlikely human behaviour. In doing so, these prose poems—a genre marked by its slipperiness and ambiguity—posit a new way of thinking about topics which are traditionally deemed unrepresentable, or even unthinkable. By attending to the margins, those shadowy places in which the separation of self and other becomes less defined, and the rules which govern a sense of order a little less clear, it might be possible to broach that which seems alien or threatening, and shape it into something that might be touched.

Acknowledgements

Many thanks to the following publications, in which a number of the prose poems in this collection have appeared in earlier forms: *antiBODY, ATOMIC, Australian Poetry Journal, Apocrypha and Abstraction Literary Journal, Best Australian Poems 2014* & *2015, Black & BLUE, The Bond Street Review, Bone Bouquet, Cider Press Review, Deletion, ditch, Duende, Eureka Street, Famous Reporter, The Grapple Annual, Jazz Cigarette, Jet Fuel Review, Malevolent Soap, Mascara Literary Review, Meniscus, Otoliths, Picaroon Poetry, Rabbit, Softblow, Snorkel, Speculative City, Sukhadia Journal of English Literature Studies, Tincture, Ucity Review, Westerly.*

Thank you to everyone who has helped in the making of this book. In particular, to the extraordinary Cassandra Atherton, for her brilliant mind, steadfast friendship, and shared joy in the abject. Your support of this manuscript has been invaluable, and I am incredibly fortunate to have had your eyes on these words. Enormous thanks to Shane Strange for understanding what I was hoping to achieve here, and for sharing the (dark, dark) vision—your editorial genius is a gift and I am thrilled to be a RWP poet; thank you for bringing this collection to life. Thank you, too, to Deakin University, which enables creative spaces and endeavours. Finally, thank you to my family and to James, three times.

About the author

Alyson Miller teaches writing and literature at Deakin University, Melbourne. Her previous collections of prose poems are *Dream Animals* (Dancing Girl Press, 2014), and *Pika-Don* (with Cassandra Atherton & Phil Day, Mountains Brown Press, 2018).

2019 Editions
Palace of Memory: An elegy **Paul Hetherington**
Acting Like a Girl **Sandra Renew**
A Coat of Ashes **Jackson**
Summer Haiku **Owen Bullock**
A Common Garment **Anita Patel**
Giant Steps **Various**
Some Sketchy Notes on Matter **Angela Gardner**
A Wardrobe of Selves **Peter Bakowski**
Breathing in Stormy Seasons **Stephanie Green**
Strange Creatures **Alyson Miller**

2018 Editions
The Uncommon Feast **Eileen Chong**
Inlandia **KA Nelson**
Peripheral Vision **Martin Dolan**
The Love of the Sun **Matt Hetherington**
Moving Targets **Jen Webb**
Things I Have Thought to Tell You Since I Saw You Last **Penelope Layland**
The Many Uses of Mint **Ravi Shankar**
Abstractions **Various**
ACE: Arresting, Contemporary stories by Emerging Writers **Various**

all titles available from
www.recentworkpress.com

www.ingramcontent.com/pod-product-compliance
Lightning Source LLC
Chambersburg PA
CBHW032051290426
44110CB00012B/1047